HAL•LEONARD
Classical
PLAY-ALONG™

Volume 17

Wolfgang Amadeus
MOZART
(1756-1791)

Piano Concerto in C Major, K 467

The Hal Leonard Classical Play-Along™ series allows you to work through great classical works systematically and at any tempo with accompaniment.

Tracks 1-3 on the CD demonstrate the concert version of each movement. Using the Amazing Slow-Downer technology included on the CD, you can adjust the recording to any tempo you like without altering the pitch. (Note that when using Amazing Slow-Downer, the CD will stop after each track instead of playing continuously.) The full cadenzas are played only in the concert version.

- Track numbers in circles ◯ – concert version
- Track numbers in diamonds ◆ – play-along version

CONCERT VERSION

Vedrana Kovac, Piano

Russian Philharmonic Orchestra Moscow

Konstantin Krimets, Conductor

T0080092

ISBN 978-1-4234-6256-9

HAL•LEONARD®
CORPORATION
7777 W. BLUEMOUND RD. P.O. BOX 13819 MILWAUKEE, WI 53213

In Australia Contact:
Hal Leonard Australia Pty. Ltd.
4 Lentara Court
Cheltenham, Victoria, 3192 Australia
Email: ausadmin@halleonard.com.au

Visit Hal Leonard Online at
www.halleonard.com

CONCERTO

for Piano in C Major, KV 467

I ①

W. A. Mozart (1756 - 1791)

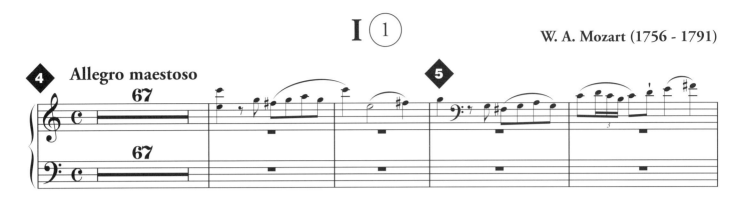

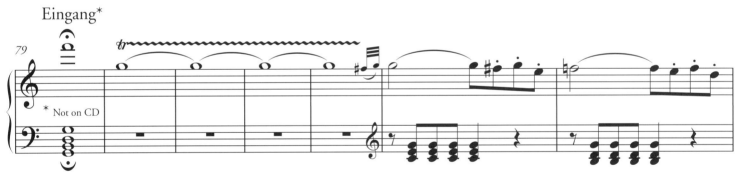

simile

Solo

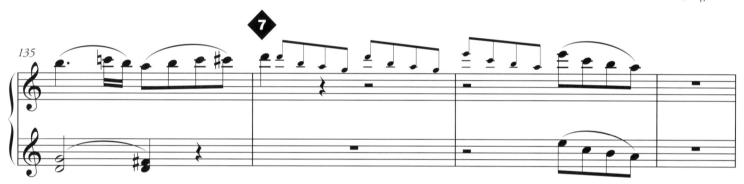

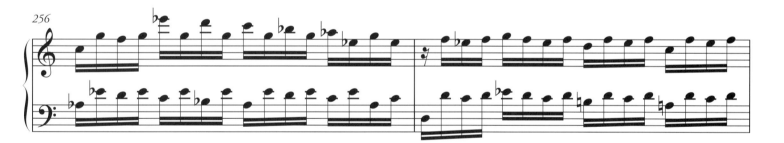

12

Cadenza

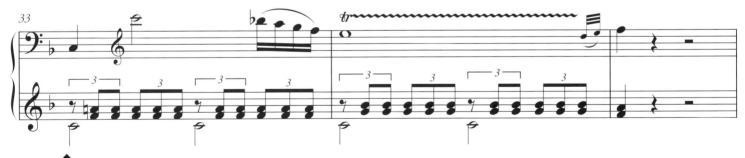

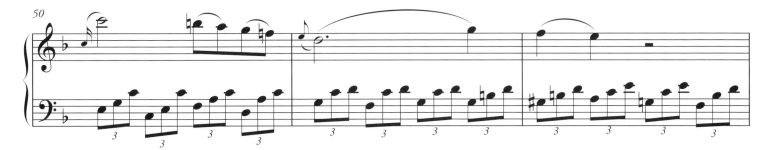

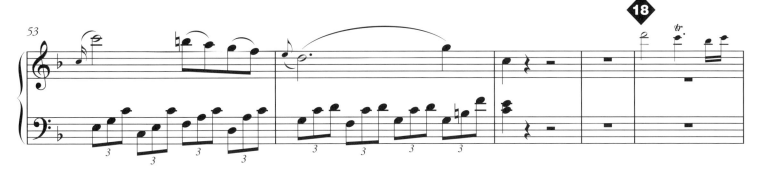

Solo

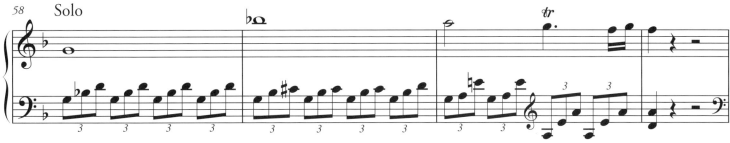

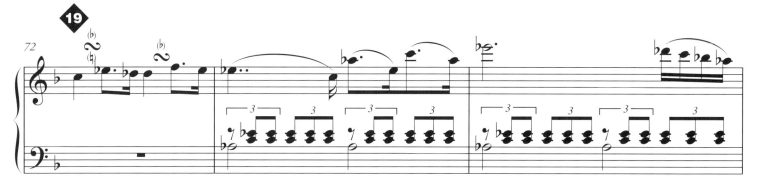

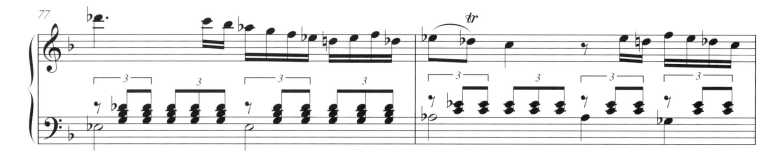

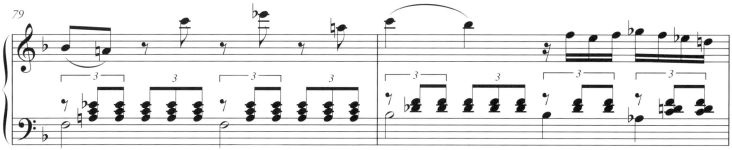

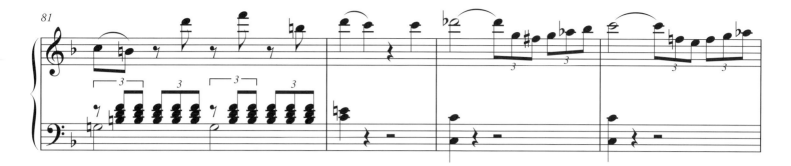

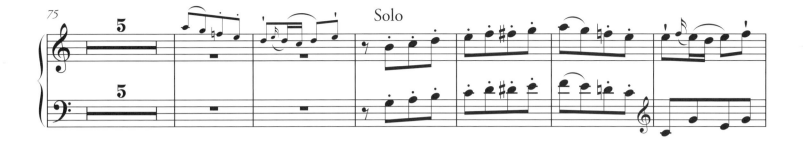

Solo

Eingang*

* Not on CD

Solo

20

20

26

Solo

4

4

Solo

Solo

Cadenza